Denver Broncos Trivia Quiz Book 2

500 More Questions On All Things Orange

Chris Bradshaw

Front cover image created by headfuzz by grimboid. Check out his great collection of TV, movie and sport-themed posters online at:

https://www.etsy.com/shop/headfuzzbygrimboid

Introduction

Welcome to the Denver Broncos Trivia Quiz Book 2. This fully revised and updated edition comes with 500 new questions on all things orange.

The format is identical to the first book. Each quiz contains 20 questions and will either be on a specific player or category, like Von Miller or quarterbacks, or will be a mixed bag on a variety of subjects.

You'll find questions on modern day stars like Chris Harris Jr., Emmanuel Sanders and Aqib Talib as well as all-time greats John Elway, Peyton Manning, Terrell Davis, Steve Atwater and many, many more.

There are questions on the Ring of Fame, Mile High Stadium, record breakers and coaches as well as the biggest games in team history. That includes the 1990s glory years as well as the triumph at Super Bowl 50.

Once again there are easy, medium and hard questions offering something for Broncos rookies as well as professors of Mile High history.

You'll find the answers to each quiz below the bottom of the following quiz. For example, the answers to Quiz 1: Pot Luck, are underneath Quiz 2: Quarterbacks. The only exception is Quiz 25: Pot Luck. The answers to these can be found under the Quiz 1 questions.

All statistics relate to the regular season only unless otherwise stated and are accurate up to the start of the 2018 season.

We hope you enjoy the Denver Broncos Trivia Quiz Book 2.

About the Author

Chris Bradshaw has written 25 quiz books including titles for Britain's biggest selling daily newspaper, The Sun, and The Times (of London). In addition to the NFL, he has written extensively on soccer, cricket, darts and poker.

He lives in Birmingham, England and has been following the Broncos for over 30 years.

Acknowledgements

Many thanks to Ken and Veronica Bradshaw, Heidi Grant, Steph, James, Ben and Will Roe and Graham Nash.

CONTENTS

Quiz 1: Pot Luck

1. Which head coach steered the Broncos to their first Super Bowl victory?

2. Who is the only player in team history to have played 16 seasons for the Broncos?

3. Demaryius Thomas was the third Bronco to catch 100 passes in a season more than once. Who were the first two?

4. Who holds the franchise record for the most regular season appearances with 236?

5. Which undrafted rookie running back caught a 29-yard touchdown pass in the 2018 season opener against Seattle?

6. Who holds the franchise record for the most sacks in a single season?

7. What number jersey is worn by defensive lineman Derek Wolfe?

8. Which Denver lineman didn't miss a single offensive snap throughout the whole of the 2015, 2016 and 2017 seasons?

9. Aqib Talib caused controversy after ripping off a chain that belonged to which receiver in a November 2017 game?

10. Who was the last Bronco to intercept 10 passes in a single season?

11. Who is the only Broncos head coach with an unbeaten playoff record?

12. Who was the last Bronco to score three rushing touchdowns in the same playoff game?

13. Whose 48-yard run gave the Broncos a famous 30-24 overtime win over New England in November 2015?

14. True or false – Emmanuel Sanders is the nephew of the great rusher Barry Sanders?

15. Head coach Vance Joseph played in the NFL in the mid-1990s for which two teams?

16. Which full back's first regular season carry resulted in a 28-yard touchdown against the Panthers in September 2016?

17. Between the 1970 NFL/AFL merger and 2017 only two teams have a better regular season record than the Broncos. Which two?

18. Which Bronco won the AP NFL Offensive Rookie of the Year Award in 2002?

19. Throughout his career John Elway threw more touchdown passes against which team than any other? a) Chiefs b) Raiders c) Seahawks

20. What nationality is defensive lineman Adam Gotsis? a) Australian b) British c) New Zealander

Quiz 25: Answers

1. Steve Atwater 2. Defensive line 3. True 4. Darrent Williams 5. Champ Bailey and Deltha O'Neal 6. Randy Gradishar 7. Aqib Talib 8. David Bruton Jr. 9. False 10. Bradley Roby 11. Julius Thomas 12. #14 13. True 14. Contact lenses 15. Ryan Harris 16. Matt Prater 17. Cincinnati 18. Darian Stewart 19. c) Cookie 20. c) 231

Quiz 2: Quarterbacks

1. Which quarterback has the most wins in Broncos history?

2. Who holds the franchise record for the most touchdown passes in a single regular season?

3. Whose 499 passing yards against the Falcons in 2004 are the most by a Broncos quarterback in a single game?

4. Which long-serving quarterback was picked by the Broncos in the 1983 NFL Draft?

5. Tim Tebow threw a game-winning 80-yard touchdown pass in a famous playoff win over which team?

6. Of Broncos quarterbacks with at least 25 starts who has the best win percentage?

7. John Elway and Peyton Manning are two of the four Denver quarterbacks to have thrown for over 4,000 yards in a season. Who are the other two?

8. True or false – Peyton Manning is the only Denver quarterback to throw more than 30 touchdown passes in a single regular season?

9. Who won more games as a starter with the Broncos – Brock Osweiler or Trevor Siemian?

10. Elway and Manning are first and second on the most completions in Broncos history list. Who is third?

11. Peyton Manning set an NFL record in the 2013 season opener against the Ravens after throwing how many touchdown passes?

12. Before Paxton Lynch, who was the last quarterback picked by the Broncos in the first round of the NFL Draft?

13. Only six quarterbacks have thrown a touchdown pass for the Broncos in a playoff game. Elway and Manning are two. Name the other four.

14. Which quarterback did the Broncos select in the first round of the 1992 NFL Draft?

15. Who threw more touchdown passes while with the Broncos – Jay Cutler or Brian Griese?

16. Who threw for a career-best 476 yards against the Colts in September 2010?

17. John Elway and Peyton Manning are first and second on the list for most career passing yards for the Broncos. Who comes next?

18. Who was the last quarterback to lead the Broncos in passing yards in a season with fewer than 2,000 yards?

19. Between 2012 and 2014 Peyton Manning threw a touchdown pass in how many straight games? a) 40 b) 42 c) 44

20. What is the highest position in the NFL Draft that the Broncos have picked a quarterback a) sixth overall b) 11th overall c) 25th overall

Quiz 1: Answers

1. Mike Shanahan 2. John Elway 3. Rod Smith and Brandon Marshall 4. Jason Elam 5. Phillip Lindsay 6. Von Miller 7. #95 8. Matt Paradis 9. Michael Crabtree 10. Champ Bailey 11. Gary Kubiak 12. Terrell Davis 13. C.J. Anderson 14. False 15. New York Jets and Indianapolis 16. Andy Janovich 17. Pittsburgh and Dallas 18. Clinton Portis 19. c) Seahawks 20. a) Australian

Quiz 3: Pot Luck

1. Who is the only special teams player to have racked up 15 years of service for the Broncos?

2. Who are the three Broncos to have won the AP NFL Most Valuable Player award?

3. Before joining the Broncos quarterback Case Keenum had played for which three franchises?

4. Who was the last tight end to lead the team in touchdowns in a single season?

5. Who was the first Broncos running back to rush for over 1,000 yards in a season?

6. Von Miller led the Broncos in sacks every year between 2011 and 2017 bar one. Who led the team in 2013?

7. In 2014, Demaryius Thomas became the third player in NFL history with over 1,400 yards and 10 or more touchdowns in three straight seasons. Who were the first two?

8. Do the Broncos have a winning or losing record in overtime games?

9. Up to the start of the 2018 season only one team had made more Super Bowl appearances than the Broncos. Which one?

10. What is the name of the horse who is the Broncos' live mascot?

11. Who holds the record for the longest field goal in team history?

12. True or false – Coach Vance Joseph was a quarterback at the University of Colorado?

13. Who recovered a crucial fumble and then delivered the game-winning sack in the 2015 Divisional round playoff game against Pittsburgh?

14. Which tight end started every game during the 2015 World Championship season?

15. During their first two seasons what color home jerseys did the Broncos wear?

16. Which rookie wide receiver threw an 80-yard touchdown pass to Cedric Tillman in a 1992 game against Dallas?

17. The Broncos delivered their last road shutout in 1992 to which now AFC North team?

18. Defensive lineman Domata Peko was born and raised on which unincorporated United States overseas territory?

19. During the 2015 World Championship season the Broncos won how many regular season games by seven points or fewer? a) seven b) eight c) nine

20. Which Super Bowl winner is the only opposition quarterback to throw seven interceptions in a game against Denver? a) Terry Bradshaw b) Trent Dilfer c) Ken Stabler

Quiz 2: Answers

1. John Elway 2. Peyton Manning 3. Jake Plummer 4. Gary Kubiak 5. Pittsburgh 6. Peyton Manning 7. Jay Cutler and Jake Plummer 8. True 9. Trevor Siemian 10. Brian Griese 11. Seven 12. Tim Tebow 13. Plummer, Morton, Tebow and DeBerg 14. Tommy Maddox 15. Brian Griese 16. Kyle Orton 17. Craig Morton 18. Tim Tebow 19. c) 44 20. b) 11th

Quiz 4: Von Miller

1. What number jersey does Miller wear?

2. In what year did Miller join the Broncos?

3. The Broncos selected Miller with which pick of the NFL Draft?

4. Miller recorded his first sack after taking down which AFC North quarterback?

5. Miller scored his first NFL touchdown returning which Tampa Bay quarterback's interception for a 26-yard score?

6. How many sacks did Miller record in his rookie season?

7. True or false – Miller has recorded at least 10 sacks in each year of his NFL career?

8. Miller returned a fumble 60 yards for a score in a 2013 game against which rival?

9. Only one player since 1982 has reached 80 sacks in fewer games than it took Miller. Which player?

10. Up to the start of the 2018 season, which quarterback had Miller sacked more than any other?

11. Miller recorded his first postseason interception in the 2015 AFC Championship game, picking off which quarterback?

12. Who was the Denver head coach when Miller was drafted?

13. Miller appeared on which TV talent show in 2016?

14. Miller was fined after performing a hip-thrusting sack dance inspired by which TV comedy duo?

15. Up to the start of the 2018 season Miller had recorded more sacks against which team than any other?

16. Miller played college ball at which southern school?

17. True or false – Miller studied agriculture at college and has his own chicken farm?

18. What is Miller's unusual middle name?

19. In what year was Miller born? a) 1988 b) 1989 c) 1990

20. What is the most sacks that Miller has recorded in a single regular season? a) 16.5 b) 17.5 c) 18.5

Quiz 3: Answers

1. Jason Elam 2. John Elway, Terrell Davis and Peyton Manning 3. Texans, Rams and Vikings 4. Julius Thomas 5. Floyd Little 6. Shaun Phillips 7. Jerry Rice and Marvin Harrison 8. Winning 9. New England 10. Thunder 11. Matt Prater 12. True 13. DeMarcus Ware 14. Owen Daniels 15. Yellow with brown numbers 16. Arthur Marshall 17. Cleveland 18. American Samoa 19. c) Nine 20. c) Ken Stabler

Quiz 5: Pot Luck

1. Which quarterback did the Broncos select with the last pick of the 2017 NFL Draft?

2. Which defensive star with Broncos connections was inducted into the Pro Football Hall of Fame in 2018?

3. Which running back's 1,502 yards in 2002 are the most in team history by a Broncos rookie?

4. Peyton Manning was given permission to wear the formerly retired Broncos #18 jersey from which quarterback?

5. With a career stretching some 15 seasons, who is the longest-serving offensive lineman in team history?

6. The Broncos signed punter Marquette King after he was released by which divisional rival?

7. Terrell Davis rushed for a postseason record 199 yards in a January 1999 game against which team?

8. In what year did the Broncos last play a regular season game that wasn't sold out?

9. Who threw more touchdown passes during the regular season of the 2015 Super Bowl-winning season – Peyton Manning or Brock Osweiler?

10. Which former Broncos offensive lineman has the same name as a baseball player who struck 555 home runs in his 19-year career?

11. True or false – Demaryius Thomas has topped 1,000 receiving yards every year since he became a Bronco?

12. Von Miller led the 2015 World Champion Broncos in sacks. Who was second on that list?

13. Who is the only Bronco to return a kickoff for a touchdown in a playoff game?

14. The Broncos signed cornerback Aqib Talib after he was released by which team?

15. Which Bronco won the AP NFL Offensive Rookie of the Year Award in 2000?

16. Which former Broncos lineman 'Clears The Air' every morning on the breakfast show on radio station 104.3FM The Fan?

17. Who are the three Denver players to have been voted to the Pro Bowl in each of their first four seasons with the team?

18. The Broncos have drafted more players from which school than any other?

19. Who holds the franchise record for the longest field goal in playoff history? a) Jason Elam b) Brandon McManus c) Matt Prater

20. Excluding strike seasons, what is the highest number of players to have suited up for the Broncos in a single season? a) 62 b) 64 c) 66

Quiz 4: Answers

1. #58 2. 2011 3. Second 4. Andy Dalton 5. Josh Freeman 6. 11.5 sacks 7. False 8. New England 9. Reggie White 10. Philip Rivers 11. Tom Brady 12. John Fox 13. Dancing With The Stars 14. Key and Peele 15. Chargers 16. Texas A & M 17. True 18. B'Vsean 19. b) 1989 20. c) 18.5 sacks

Quiz 6: Ring of Fame

Identify the Ring of Fame player from the descriptions below.

1. This tough offensive lineman was named on the NFL All-Decade teams for the 1980s and 1990s.

2. This star running back led the team in rushing for seven straight seasons in the late 1960s and early 1970s.

3. This talkative tight end won a Super Bowl ring with Baltimore as well as two with the Broncos.

4. One of the hardest hitters in NFL history, this defensive back picked off 24 passes between 1989 and 1998.

5. Another tough-tackling defensive back, this USC graduate made 170 starts between 1981 and 1994.

6. This impressive pass rusher became just the 11th player in NFL history to record 100 sacks for a single team.

7. This linebacker holds the team record for the most tackles in a single season after registering 286 in 1978.

8. This Louisville linebacker, picked in the fourth round of the 1974 draft, went on to play 191 games for the Broncos.

9. This Hawaii grad holds the team record for the most field goals in team history with 395.

10. This linebacker is the only player in Broncos history to register four sacks in a single game more than once.

11. This head coach steered the Broncos to their first appearance in the Super Bowl.

12. This former Cowboy and Giant is third on the list of most wins by a Broncos quarterback.

13. Picked in the seventh round of the 1994 NFL Draft, this lineman went on to appear in 194 games for the Broncos.

14. This undrafted free agent went on to become the Broncos' all-time leading receiver.

15. This speedy receiver was the first Bronco to amass over 1,000 receiving yards in a single season.

16. This kicker scored 742 points during nine seasons with the Broncos in the 1970s.

17. This running back's 142.5 yards per game in playoff games is an NFL record.

18. This defensive tackle was a key part of the Orange Crush defense and registered 55.5 sacks between 1968 and 1978.

19. This long-time Tampa Bay defensive back spent the final four years of his pro career with the Broncos between 2004 and 2007.

20. This returner scored eight punt return touchdowns for the Broncos between 1975 and 1983.

Quiz 5: Answers

1. Chad Kelly 2. Brian Dawkins 3. Clinton Portis 4. Frank Tripucka 5. Tom Nalen 6. Oakland 7. Miami 8. 1970 9. Brock Osweiler 10. Manny Ramirez 11. False 12. DeMarcus Ware 13. Trindon Holliday 14. New England 15. Mike Anderson 16. Mark Schlereth 17. Champ Bailey, Aqib Talib and John Lynch 18. University of Florida 19. c) Matt Prater 20. c) 66

Quiz 7: Pot Luck

1. Derek Wolfe was only the second Broncos defensive lineman to start all 16 games in his rookie year. Who was the first? (clue: it was in 1973)

2. At 5ft 5in tall, which explosive returner is the shortest player to have appeared for the Broncos in franchise history?

3. True or false – The Broncos have never won the Super Bowl wearing orange jerseys?

4. Who is second behind Terrell Davis in career rushing yards for the Broncos?

5. Running back Phillip Lindsay played college ball for which team?

6. Which college played host to the Broncos' training camp between 1982 and 2002?

7. Before Von Miller, who was the last Bronco to record double digit sacks in back-to-back seasons?

8. Who recorded seven tackles, a pass defended, a fumble recovery, and an interception in Super Bowl 50?

9. True or false – Under Pat Bowlen's ownership the Broncos have been to more Super Bowls than had losing seasons?

10. Do the Broncos have a winning or losing record in season-opening games?

11. In 2011, who became the first Broncos punter in over 40 years to punt over 100 times in a season?

12. Who picked off a Dak Prescott pass in September 2017 and returned it 103 yards for a touchdown?

13. In which round of the 2018 NFL Draft did the Broncos select running back Royce Freeman?

14. Who were the only two Broncos elected to the Pro Bowl following the hugely disappointing 2017 season?

15. Terrell Davis holds the team record for the most rushing touchdowns in playoff games. Who is second on that list?

16. Who led the team with three picks during the 2015 regular season?

17. Who is the only Bronco to have won the AP NFL Defensive Player of the Year award?

18. Which opposition pass rusher recorded five sacks in a 2015 game against the Broncos?

19. How many points did the World Champion Broncos score during the 2015 regular season? a) 345 b) 355 c) 365

20. Which former Bronco appeared in the 2018 edition of the TV show 'Dancing With The Stars'? a) Peyton Manning b) Evan Mathis c) DeMarcus Ware

Quiz 6: Answers

1. Gary Zimmerman 2. Floyd Little 3. Shannon Sharpe 4. Steve Atwater 5. Dennis Smith 6. Simon Fletcher 7. Randy Gradishar 8. Tom Jackson 9. Jason Elam 10. Karl Mecklenburg 11. Red Miller 12. Craig Morton 13. Tom Nalen 14. Rod Smith 15. Lionel Taylor 16. Jim Turner 17. Terrell Davis 18. Paul Smith 19. John Lynch 20. Rick Upchurch

Quiz 8: 1997 World Champions

1. The Broncos clinched their first world championship after defeating which team in Super Bowl XXXII?

2. What was the score in that game?

3. Which city hosted Super Bowl XXXII?

4. True or false – The Broncos were an 11-point underdog going into Super Bowl XXXII?

5. The half time show at Super Bowl XXXII featured a tribute to which famous record label?

6. Who was the starting center on the Super Bowl XXXII team?

7. The 1997 team finished the regular season with what win/loss record?

8. What was the only NFC team to defeat the Broncos throughout the whole of the 1997 season?

9. Terrell Davis led the team in rushing yards in 1997. Which back, who was better known as a kick returner, was second on the rushing list?

10. Which pair of Broncos had over 1,000 receiving yards during the 1997 season?

11. Who returned three punts for touchdowns during the 1997 season?

12. Who was the only defensive player on the 1997 team to receive First Team All-Pro honors?

13. True or false – The Broncos had lost regular season games against the teams they faced in the Divisional Round and AFC Championship games?

14. Shannon Sharpe was one of two tight ends to catch a touchdown pass for the Broncos during the 1997 season. Who was the other?

15. Which 2018 NFL head coach was a member of the Broncos' Super Bowl XXXII roster?

16. In the Wild Card round the Broncos had two rushers break the 100-yard mark. Terrell Davis was one, who was the other?

17. Which team won the AFC West in 1997?

18. Who was the team's offensive coordinator in 1997?

19. Which NFC South opponent did the Broncos rout 34-0 midway through the 1997 season? a) Atlanta b) Carolina c) New Orleans

20. The Broncos led the NFL in points scored in 1997, racking up how many during the regular season? a) 452 b) 462 c) 472

Quiz 7: Answers

1. Barney Chavous 2. Trindon Holliday 3. True 4. Floyd Little 5. Colorado Buffs 6. University of Northern Colorado 7. Trevor Pryce 8. T.J Ward 9. True 10. Winning 11. Britton Colquitt 12. Aqib Talib 13. Third 14. Von Miller and Aqib Talib 15. John Elway 16. Aqib Talib 17. Randy Gradishar 18. Khalil Mack 19. b) 355 20. c) DeMarcus Ware

Quiz 9: Pot Luck

1. Which quarterback, who played with the Broncos in 1995 and 1996, was named the team's offensive coordinator in November 2017?

2. With which pick of the 2018 NFL Draft did the Broncos select Bradley Chubb?

3. Which team did the Broncos defeat in their most recent overtime playoff win?

4. Before Garett Bolles in 2017 who was the last offensive lineman selected by the Broncos in the first round of the NFL Draft?

5. Do the Broncos have a winning or losing record in games played on artificial turf?

6. Which linebacker won the AP NFL Defensive Rookie of the Year Award in 1991?

7. Which quarterback holds the franchise record for the most 300-yard passing games in a single season?

8. What does the initial T stand for in the name of former defensive star T.J. Ward?

9. True or false – Between 1962 and 1966 the Broncos wore orange helmets?

10. In what year did the Broncos win their first AFC West title?

11. Before Demaryius Thomas who was the last Bronco to catch 100 passes in a single season?

12. Throughout the whole of the 1980s the Broncos had just two backs who rushed for 1,000 yards in a season. Which two?

13. Which Denver safety was elected to the Pro Bowl for the first time in his career after an impressive 2016 season?

14. Peyton Manning and John Elway are two of the three Broncos quarterbacks to have passed for over 300 yards in a playoff game. Who is the third?

15. True or false – Brandon McManus was a perfect 10 for 10 on his first 10 postseason field goal attempts?

16. Which offensive lineman appears on Twitter using the moniker @two_dice?

17. Twice during the 1980s the Broncos used a first-round draft pick to select a running back. Which pair did they choose?

18. In what round of the 2014 NFL Draft did the Broncos select cornerback Bradley Roby?

19. Who was the only defensive back to start every game during the 2015 World Championship season? a) Chris Harris Jr b) Aqib Talib c) T.J. Ward

20. Former offensive lineman Cyrus Kouandjio was the first player from which African country to play for the Broncos? a) Cameroon b) Kenya c) Nigeria

Quiz 8: Answers

1. Green Bay 2. Broncos 31-24 Packers 3. San Diego 4. True 5. Motown 6. Tom Nalen 7. 12-4 8. San Francisco 9. Vaughn Hebron 10. Rod Smith and Shannon Sharpe 11. Darrien Gordon 12. John Mobley 13. True 14. Dwayne Carswell 15. Anthony Lynn 16. Derek Loville 17. Kansas City 18. Gary Kubiak 19. b) Carolina 20. c) 472

Quiz 10: 1998 World Champions

1. The Broncos claimed their second Lombardi Trophy after defeating which team in Super Bowl XXXIII?

2. What was the score in the big game?

3. Super Bowl XXXIII was hosted in which state?

4. Who was named the game's Most Valuable Player?

5. Which two Broncos scored rushing touchdowns in Super Bowl XXXIII?

6. Who was the only Bronco with a touchdown reception in Super Bowl XXXIII?

7. Which Bronco picked off two passes in Super Bowl XXXIII, returning one of them 58 yards?

8. Who was the referee at Super Bowl XXXIII?

9. How many games did the Broncos win during the 1998 regular season?

10. How many yards did Terrell Davis rush for during his record-breaking 1998 regular season?

11. Which NFC team ended the Broncos' unbeaten start to the 1998 season?

12. Which three offensive linemen on the 1998 team received Pro Bowl honors?

13. Who were the two defensive players on the 1998 team to receive Pro Bowl recognition?

14. Which Super Bowl XXXIII-starter had a surname that ended with the letter Z?

15. The Broncos turned a 0-10 deficit into a 24-10 victory over which team in the AFC Championship game?

16. Which backup quarterback steered the Broncos to four straight wins in relief of an injured John Elway during the 1998 season?

17. Who was the only running back other than Terrell Davis to total 100 yards during the whole of the 1998 regular season?

18. Which long-time Denver linebacker and future offensive coordinator was a special teams-coach on the 1998 team?

19. How many points did the Broncos rack up in the 1998 regular season? a) 481 b) 491 c) 501

20. What was the only AFC team to defeat the Broncos during the 1998 season? a) Buffalo b) Miami c) New England

Quiz 9: Answers

1. Bill Musgrave 2. Fifth 3. Pittsburgh 4. Ryan Clady 5. Losing 6. Mike Croel 7. Peyton Manning 8. Terrell 9. True 10. 1977 11. Brandon Marshall 12. Sammy Winder and Bobby Humphrey 13. Darian Stewart 14. Tim Tebow 15. True 16. Matt Paradis 17. Gerald Willhite and Steve Sewell 18. First 19. Chris Harris Jr. 20. a) Cameroon

Quiz 11: Pot Luck

1. Do the Broncos have a winning or losing record on Monday Night Football?

2. Defensive coordinator Joe Woods spent his first two seasons in Denver coaching which position group?

3. Who is second behind John Elway on the list of most starts by a Broncos player?

4. Which running back's 5,427 rushing yards between 1982 and 1990 put him in third place on the Broncos' all-time list?

5. Between 1989 and 1993 only one player in the NFL registered more sacks than Denver's Simon Fletcher. Which one?

6. What specialist position was held by Casey Kreiter on the Broncos' 2017 roster?

7. The coldest ever game involving the Broncos saw temperatures drop to zero at which stadium?

8. Who is the only Denver receiver to pass 100-receiving yards three times in his rookie season?

9. Emmanuel Sanders caught a hat-trick of touchdown passes in a 2014 win over which divisional rival?

10. True or false – The Broncos have never scored an interception return touchdown in the playoffs?

11. Since 1970, only one team has a better home field advantage in regular season games than the Broncos. Which one?

12. Who were the two Broncos to gain 1,000 or more receiving yards in a single season during the 1980s?

13. The Broncos delivered their first shutout in 12 years during the 2017 season, defeating which AFC East team 23-0?

14. Which Kansas City slinger is the only opposition quarterback to throw six touchdown passes in a single game against the Broncos?

15. The Broncos have had two 6'7" quarterbacks in team history. Can you name the pair?

16. Who are the three Denver backs to have rushed for over 100 yards in a single playoff game?

17. Who tied an NFL record after converting five field goals in a 2015 playoff game against the Steelers?

18. True or false – Peyton Manning was the first starting quarterback to win the Super Bowl with two different teams?

19. During the 2015 World Championship season which defensive star played the most snaps? a) Chris Harris Jr b) Von Miller c) Aqib Talib

20. Former offensive lineman Menelik Watson was born and raised in which country? a) England b) Germany c) Nigeria

Quiz 10: Answers

1. Atlanta 2. Broncos 34-19 Atlanta 3. Florida 4. John Elway 5. John Elway and Howard Griffith 6. Rod Smith 7. Darrien Gordon 8. Bernie Kukar 9. 14 games 10. 2,008 yards 11. New York Giants 12. Tom Nalen, Mark Schlereth and Tony Jones 13. Steve Atwater and Bill Romanowski 14. Glenn Cadrez 15. New York Jets 16. Bubby Brister 17. Derek Loville 18. Rick Dennison 19. c) 501 20. b) Miami

Quiz 12: 2015 World Champions

1. Which team did the Broncos face in Super Bowl 50?

2. What was the final score in the game?

3. Who was named the game's Most Valuable Player?

4. Super Bowl 50 was hosted at which stadium?

5. Which defensive lineman scored Denver's first touchdown in Super Bowl 50?

6. Who scored the Broncos' only offensive touchdown in Super Bowl 50?

7. Which defensive back recorded Denver's only interception in Super Bowl 50?

8. True or false – The Broncos were five-point underdogs heading into Super Bowl 50?

9. How many sacks did the Broncos defense record in Super Bowl 50?

10. The Broncos started their playoff run with a 23-16 win over which team?

11. Denver reached Super Bowl 50 after beating which team in the AFC Championship decider?

12. The Broncos finished the regular season with what win / loss record?

13. The Broncos started the 2017 season with how many straight wins?

14. Complete the famous phrase uttered by John Elway when collecting the trophy at Super Bowl 50. "This one's for..."?

15. Who led the team in rushing yards during the 2015 regular season?

16. Peyton Manning's final pass was a two-point conversion in Super Bowl 50 that was caught by which receiver?

17. Which English band headlined the half-time show at Super Bowl 50?

18. Which female singer performed the national anthem at Super Bowl 50?

19. How many games during the 2015 season did the Broncos win with Brock Osweiler as the starting quarterback? a) four b) five c) six

20. How many points did the Broncos give up during the 2015 regular season? a) 286 b) 296 c) 306

Quiz 11: Answers

1. Losing 2. Defensive backs 3. Tom Nalen 4. Sammy Winder 5. Reggie White 6. Long snapper 7. Arrowhead 8. Eddie Royal 9. San Diego 10. True 11. Pittsburgh 12. Steve Watson and Vance Johnson 13. New York Jets 14. Len Dawson 15. Brock Osweiler and Paxton Lynch 16. Terrell Davis, Sammy Winder and Derek Loville 17. Brandon McManus 18. True 19. a) Chris Harris Jr 20. a) England

Quiz 13: Pot Luck

1. Up to the start of the 2018 season the Broncos had had how many permanent head coaches?

2. Do the Broncos have a winning or losing record in Sunday Night Football games?

3. John Fox's final game as head coach was a 24-12 playoff loss to which team?

4. The Netflix animation 'Kulipari: An Army of Frogs' is based on a character created by which former Denver defensive star?

5. The Broncos blocked an extra point which was then returned for a 2-point score to give them a dramatic 25-23 win in 2016 over which NFC South team?

6. Which rookie safety blocked that famous extra point?

7. And which rookie safety returned the blocked kick for the game-winning score?

8. Between 1997 and 1998 the Broncos won how many straight games (including the postseason)?

9. True or false – The Broncos have never won a postseason game played on artificial turf?

10. Who was the last Bronco to lead the team in tackles in back-to-back seasons?

11. Who were the four Denver receivers to amass 1,000 or more receiving yards in a season in the 1990s?

12. After spending five seasons with the Colts, who was appointed the Broncos' special-teams coordinator in 2018?

13. Of Broncos quarterbacks to have thrown at least 45 postseason passes who is the only one not to throw an interception?

14. Who was the last Broncos first-round draft pick whose surname starts with a vowel?

15. True or false – Since 1984, the Broncos have appeared in more AFC Championship games then the rest of their AFC West rivals combined?

16. What number jersey does quarterback Case Keenum wear?

17. Who was the referee at Super Bowl 50?

18. What color is the mane on the Broncos' logo?

19. Which team have the Broncos shut out the most times in franchise history? a) Chargers b) Chiefs c) Raiders

20. Up to the start of the 2018 season, how many different players had appeared for the Broncos in regular and postseason play in team history? a) 1,302 b) 1,402 c) 1,502

Quiz 12: Answers

1. Carolina 2. Broncos 24-10 Panthers 3. Von Miller 4. Levi's Stadium 5. Malik Jackson 6. C.J. Anderson 7. T.J. Ward 8. True 9. Seven 10. Pittsburgh 11. New England 12. 12-4 13. Seven 14. Pat 15. Ronnie Hillman 16. Bennie Fowler 17. Coldplay 18. Lady Gaga 19. b) Five 20. b) 296

Quiz 14: Record Breakers

1. Which defender played in 172 consecutive games between 1985 and 1995?

2. In October 1963, Don Stone became the first Bronco to do what?

3. Who holds the record for the most 100-yard receiving games in franchise history?

4. The Broncos played in front of a record crowd of 101,063 in Super Bowl XXI. Which stadium hosted that game?

5. Despite being down 0-24 with just 24 seconds of the third quarter remaining, the Broncos went on to beat which team 35-24 in October 2012?

6. Who set a franchise record after rushing for 188 yards in the first half of a 2003 game against the Chiefs?

7. Who are the two defensive players with 14 years of active service for the Broncos?

8. John Elway holds the team record for the most starts in playoff games. Who is second on that list?

9. Which journeyman backup quarterback set the franchise record for the most consecutive completions in 1994 with 21?

10. Who holds the team record for the most receiving yards in a single game?

11. Which defensive lineman, who played in Denver from 1980 through to 1988, holds the team record for the most safeties with three?

12. Who holds the record for the most postseason interceptions in team history with five in the late 1990s?

13. Who set the record for the longest punt in team history in 1984 after booming an 84-yarder against the Chiefs?

14. In 2005, the Broncos became the first team in NFL history with two 100-yard rushers and a 300-yard passer in the same game. Who were the record-breaking running backs and quarterback who set that record?

15. Who holds the team record for the most field goals by a Broncos kicker in playoff games?

16. Which three-time Pro Bowl cornerback started a record 156 straight games for the Broncos between 1971 and 1981?

17. The longest pass in team history that didn't result in a touchdown was an 88-yarder from Brian Griese to which tight end?

18. John Elway threw more touchdown passes to which receiver than any other?

19. Including the postseason, Terrell Davis broke the 100-yard rushing barrier in how many games? a) 31 b) 41 c) 51

20. In 1997 the Broncos set a postseason record after rushing for 310 yards in a game against which team? a) Packers b) Jags c) Jets

Quiz 13: Answers

1. 12 2. Winning 3. Indianapolis 4. Trevor Pryce 5. New Orleans 6. Justin Simmons 7. Will Parks 8. 18 games 9. False – they're 1-10 10. D.J. Williams 11. Anthony Miller, Rod Smith, Shannon Sharpe, Ed McCaffrey 12. Tom McMahon 13. Tim Tebow 14. Robert Ayers 15. True 16. #4 17. Clete Blakeman 18. Orange 19. a) Chargers 20. a) 1,302

Quiz 15: Pot Luck

1. What important place in team history is held by a man called Ward M Vining?

2. At the start of the 2018 season, who was the longest tenured Bronco having joined the team in 2010?

3. The Broncos lost how many straight games during the middle of the 2017 season?

4. Before Bradley Roby in 2014, who was the last cornerback selected by the Broncos in the first round of the NFL Draft?

5. Veteran offensive lineman Ron Leary spent the first six years of his NFL career with which team?

6. Which Bronco was named the NFL Special Teams Player of the Year in 2001?

7. The Broncos were routed by a score of 43-8 in a Super Bowl XLVIII loss to which team?

8. Who were the two Denver backs to rush for over 1,000 yards in a season during the 1970s?

9. Who was the last Denver receiver with at least 20 catches to average over 20 yards per catch in a single season?

10. Which Green Bay back rushed for a 98-yard touchdown in December 2003, the longest given up by the Broncos defense in team history?

11. True or false – The Broncos have never won a game on Thanksgiving Day?

12. Between 1996 and 1998 the Broncos won how many home regular season games in succession?

13. In 2018 the Broncos traded quarterback Trevor Siemian to which team?

14. Who is the only Bronco with 200 receiving yards in a single postseason game?

15. Which Broncos defender appears on Twitter under the username @astronaut?

16. In the 1960s the Broncos played a couple of home games at the stadium of which college?

17. Which Bronco was the first undrafted player in league history to pass 100 scrimmage yards in both of his first two NFL appearances?

18. Who returned a Tom Brady interception 100 yards but didn't quite score in the 2005 Divisional playoff?

19. What is the most points that the Broncos have scored in a single playoff game? a) 41 b) 42 c) 43

20. Between 2011 and 2015 the Broncos won how many straight divisional road games? a) 13 b) 14 c) 15

Quiz 14: Answers

1. Simon Fletcher 2. Rush for 100 yards in a game 3. Demaryius Thomas 4. Rose Bowl, Pasadena 5. San Diego 6. Clinton Portis 7. Tom Jackson and Dennis Smith 8. Steve Atwater 9. Hugh Millen 10. Demaryius Thomas 11. Rulon Jones 12. Darrien Gordon 13. Chris Norman 14. Mike Anderson, Tatum Bell and Jake Plummer 15. Jason Elam 16. Bill Thompson 17. Byron Chamberlain 18. Shannon Sharpe 19. b) 41 20. b) Jags

Quiz 16: Mile High Magic

1. Did the Broncos have a winning or losing record at Mile High Stadium?

2. The Broncos reached Super Bowl XXII after a famous 38-33 win at Mile High Stadium over which team?

3. How many touchdown passes did John Elway throw at Mile High Stadium?

4. Which receiver's 95-yard reception against Detroit in 1981 was the longest touchdown catch at Mile High Stadium?

5. True or false – The Colorado Rockies spent two seasons playing home games at Mile High Stadium?

6. In what year did the Broncos play their final home game at Mile High Stadium?

7. The Broncos signed off from Mile High Stadium with a resounding 38-9 victory over which NFC team?

8. Denver opened Broncos Stadium at Mile High with a 31-20 win over which NFC East team?

9. In 2013, the Broncos scored 52 points (a record at Broncos Stadium at Mile High) against which NFC team?

10. What is the name of the horse statue that appears above the scoreboard at Broncos Stadium at Mile High?

11. True or false – That horse statue was modelled on Roy Rogers' famous horse Trigger?

12. Do the Broncos have a winning or losing record at Broncos Stadium at Mile High?

13. Which financial company was the first sponsor of Broncos Stadium at Mile High?

14. Which retailer took over the stadium sponsorship in 2011?

15. Which quarterback holds the record for the most passing yards in a single game at Broncos Stadium at Mile High?

16. Who holds the record for the most rushing yards by a Broncos back in a game at Broncos Stadium at Mile High?

17. The first public event staged at Broncos Stadium at Mile High was a concert by which legendary rock band? (clue: Their name is the same as an NFL team's nickname)

18. In 2018 Broncos Stadium at Mile High played host to a rugby league international between England and which country?

19. What is the seating capacity of Broncos Stadium at Mile High? a) 74,125 b) 75,125 c) 76,125

20. By what name was Mile High Stadium originally known? a) Bears Stadium b) Broncos Stadium c) Cowboys Stadium

Quiz 15: Answers

1. He came up with the Broncos nickname 2. Demaryius Thomas 3. Eight 4. Willie Middlebrooks 5. Dallas 6. Jason Elam 7. Seattle 8. Floyd Little and Otis Armstrong 9. Ashley Lelie 10. Ahman Green 11. False 12. 24 games 13. Minnesota 14. Demaryius Thomas 15. Bradley Chubb 16. Denver University 17. Phillip Lindsay 18. Champ Bailey 19. b) 42 points 20. c) 15

Quiz 17: Pot Luck

1. Who was the last Bronco to rush for over 100 yards in a playoff game?

2. Who led the team in sacks every year between 1988 and 1994?

3. Which receiver's first NFL reception was a 43-yard touchdown as time expired that gave the Broncos a 38-31 win over Washington in September 1995?

4. The first name of which linebacker, who made his Broncos debut in 2016, is the same as the former name of the country now known as the Democratic Republic of the Congo?

5. Which Bronco was named the AP NFL Defensive Rookie of the Year in 2011?

6. Who was last non-kicker to lead the team in scoring?

7. The Broncos scored four touchdowns of 40 yards or more in a 2007 game against which AFC South team?

8. In what year did Pat Bowlen assume ownership of the Broncos franchise?

9. Former kicker Jason Elam wore what number jersey?

10. True or false – The real first name of former linebacker D.J. Williams is Genos?

11. Before becoming a member of the Broncos' all-conquering defense, T.J. Ward spent the first four years of his career with which team?

12. After controversially being released by the Broncos Ward signed for which NFC team?

13. Safety Darian Stewart joined the Broncos as a free agent after being released by which team?

14. If all the players to have played for the Broncos were listed alphabetically who would be last on the list?

15. True or false – The Broncos have never gone through a whole game without giving away a penalty?

16. Who are the two Broncos receivers with 14 catches in a single playoff game?

17. Who is the only Bronco to return a punt for a touchdown in a playoff game?

18. Which divisional rival defeated the Broncos 33-10 on Christmas Day 2016?

19. In a must-win 2015 season finale, Peyton Manning came off the bench at half time to steer the Broncos to a 27-20 victory over which team? a) Chargers b) Chiefs c) Raiders

20. Alex Gibbs was a legendary coach of which position group? a) defensive line b) linebackers c) offensive line

Quiz 16: Answers

1. Winning 2. Cleveland 3. 180 4. Steve Watson 5. True 6. 2000 7. San Francisco 8. New York Giants 9. Philadelphia 10. Bucky 11. True 12. Winning 13. Invesco 14. Sports Authority 15. Jake Plummer 16. Clinton Portis 17. The Eagles 18. New Zealand 19. c) 76,125 20. b) Bears Stadium

Quiz 18: Coaches

1. Which alliteratively-named coach was the first head coach in Broncos history?

2. Excluding interim appointments, which head coach has the best overall winning percentage?

3. Who are the two Denver head coaches with over 100 wins?

4. Who won more games while head coach of the Broncos – Wade Phillips or Josh McDaniels?

5. Which head coach steered the team to victory in Super Bowl 50?

6. Who are the two Broncos head coaches to go 6-0 in their first six games?

7. Who was the defensive coordinator on the 2015 World Championship team?

8. Who holds the record for the most playoff wins as head coach of the Broncos?

9. Before becoming the Broncos head coach Gary Kubiak had been offensive coordinator at which team?

10. Which former Bronco was offensive coordinator under Mike Shanahan from 2006 until 2008 then again under Gary Kubiak in 2015 and 2016?

11. Including spells as an assistant and head coach, who is Denver's longest serving coach?

12. Which offensive coordinator steered the Broncos to their highest even points haul during the 2013 season?

13. The Denver offensive and defensive coordinators in 2012 both went on to become head coaches of AFC West teams. Name the pair.

14. Who succeeded Dan Reeves as the Broncos head coach?

15. How many games did the Broncos win in Mike Shanahan's first season as head coach?

16. Who was the first African-American head coach of the Broncos, albeit on an interim basis?

17. What was Red Miller's real first name?

18. Who was the Broncos' defensive coordinator from 1972 through to 1988?

19. Which Broncos head coach suffered the most playoff losses? a) John Fox b) Dan Reeves c) Mike Shanahan

20. Which of the following coaches had the most wins as Broncos head coach? a) John Fox b) Gary Kubiak c) Wade Phillips

Quiz 17: Answers

1. Terrell Davis in 1999 2. Simon Fletcher 3. Rod Smith 4. Zaire (Anderson) 5. Von Miller 6. Julius Thomas 7. Tennessee 8. 1984 9. #1 10. True 11. Cleveland 12. Tampa Bay 13. Baltimore 14. Gary Zimmerman 15. False 16. Shannon Sharpe and Demaryius Thomas 17. Trindon Holliday 18. Kansas City 19. a) Chargers 20. c) Offensive line

Quiz 19: Pot Luck

1. Who are the three Broncos to have earned Pro Bowl honors in six of their first seven seasons with the team?

2. 2018 first round draft pick Bradley Chubb played college ball at which school?

3. Who was the last running back selected by the Broncos in the first round of the NFL Draft?

4. Which Bronco co-wrote the 2018 book 'Playing for More: Trust Beyond What You Can See'?

5. Who are the two wide receiver tandems to have recorded 1,000-yard seasons three years in a row?

6. In what year did the Broncos play their 500th regular season game?

7. Which linebacker is the Broncos' all-time leader in tackles?

8. Terrell Davis holds the franchise record for the most touchdowns in a season with 23. Who, with 17 in 2002, is second on that list?

9. Who was the last Bronco with at least 100 rushing attempts to average over 5 yards per carry in a season?

10. Who was the owner of the Broncos immediately prior to Pat Bowlen?

11. True or false – The Broncos didn't record back-to-back losing seasons between 1973 and 2017?

12. Which of the famous trio of receivers known as 'The Three Amigos' was a first-round draft pick?

13. Which Broncos head coach appeared in Super Bowls V and VI as a player?

14. Which Cincinnati back rushed for 278 yards in October 2000, the most given up by the Broncos in a single game in team history?

15. Who holds the record for the most catches by a Broncos player in playoff games?

16. Who set a game record after returning a punt 61 yards in Super Bowl 50?

17. @MOOCHIE048 is the Twitter handle of which Broncos defender?

18. True or False – The 1998 Broncos allowed just 28 rushing yards in the AFC Divisional Round and Championship Game combined?

19. What as Champ Bailey's real first name? a) Robert b) Ronnie c) Roland

20. Linebacker Shaq Barrett played college ball at which school? a) Air Force b) Colorado c) Colorado State

Quiz 18: Answers

1. Frank Filchock 2. John Fox 3. Mike Shanahan and Dan Reeves 4. Wade Phillips 5. Gary Kubiak 6. McDaniels and Kubiak 7. Wade Phillips 8. Mike Shanahan 9. Baltimore 10. Rick Dennison 11. Mike Shanahan 12. Adam Gase 13. Mike McCoy and Jack Del Rio 14. Wade Phillips 15. Eight 16. Eric Studesville 17. Robert 18. Joe Collier 19. b) Dan Reeves 20. a) John Fox

Quiz 20: Nicknames

1. The Duke   A) Terrance Knighton

2. TD   B) Mark Schlereth

3. The Sheriff   C) T.J. Ward

4. The Chinese Dragon   D) Howard Griffith

5. Pot Roast   E) Wade Phillips

6. Pacman   F) Brian Dawkins

7. The Smiling Assassin   G) Dwayne Carswell

8. The Snow Goose   H) John Elway

9. Tombstone   I) Terrell Davis

10. Kool   J) Tyrone Braxton

11. Stink   K) Von Miller

12. The Snake   L) Peyton Manning

13. Boss   M) Rich Jackson

14. Chicken   N) Brandon Stokley

15. House   O) Austin Gonsoulin

16. Weapon X   P) Steve Atwater

17. Son of Bum   Q) Adam Jones

18. Goose   R) Karl Mecklenburg

19. The Human Plow   S) Jake Plummer

20. The Slot Machine   T) Elvis Dumervil

Quiz 19: Answers

1. Steve Atwater, Champ Bailey and Von Miller 2. North Carolina State 3. Knowshon Moreno 4. Case Keenum 5. Rod Smith and Ed McCaffrey and Demaryius Thomas and Emmanuel Sanders 6. 1994 7. Randy Gradishar 8. Clinton Portis 9. Tim Tebow 10. Edgar Kaiser 11. True 12. Ricky Nattiel 13. Dan Reeves 14. Corey Dillon 15. Demaryius Thomas 16. Jordan Norwood 17. Shaq Barrett 18. True 19. c) Roland 20. c) Colorado State

Quiz 21: Pot Luck

1. Who holds the record for the most double-digit sack seasons in franchise history?

2. Prior to the start of the 2018 season, who was the last Bronco to rush for over 200 yards in a game?

3. Before Garett Bolles in 2017, who was the last left tackle to start all 16 games in his rookie season?

4. What color helmet did the Broncos wear in their first two seasons?

5. The Broncos have never played a competitive game on which two days of the week?

6. Appearing for 14 seasons between 1981 and 1994, who is Denver's longest serving defensive back?

7. Simon Fletcher is one of two players in NFL history to register a sack in 10 straight games. Which pass rusher, who also has Denver connections, is the other?

8. Temperatures reached a record 103F during a 2001 game at which NFC opponent?

9. Between 1984 and 2017 only one team enjoyed more regular season wins than the Broncos. Which one?

10. In 2005, who became the first Broncos punter to be named AFC Special Teams Player of the Month?

11. Which running back led the team in touchdowns during the 2015 World Championship season?

12. Who are the two Broncos with at least 1,500 receiving yards in a single season?

13. Which city in Nebraska was often heard when Peyton Manning was calling an audible?

14. Who are the three Broncos to have made the Pro Bowl in five straight seasons?

15. Niamiah is the middle name of which Broncos receiver?

16. The largest regular season crowd the Broncos have played in front of was in a 2013 game at which team?

17. Which tight end caught two touchdown passes in the 2015 AFC Championship game?

18. True or false – Broncos Stadium at Mile High is designed in the shape of a horse shoe?

19. What is the largest home attendance in franchise history? a) 75,160 b) 76,160 c) 77,160

20. That record crowd assembled for a 2007 game against which team? a) Chicago b) Detroit c) Green Bay

Quiz 20: Answers

1. John Elway 2. Terrell Davis 3. Peyton Manning 4. Von Miller 5. Terrance Knighton 6. Adam Jones 7. Steve Atwater 8. Karl Mecklenburg 9. Rich Jackson 10. Elvis Dumervil 11. Mark Schlereth 12. Jake Plummer 13. T.J. Ward 14. Tyrone Braxton 15. Dwayne Carswell 16. Brian Dawkins 17. Wade Phillips 18. Austin Gonsoulin 19. Howard Griffith 20. Brandon Stokley

Quiz 22: Numbers Game

Identify the jersey number worn by the following players.

1. Otis Armstrong and Champ Bailey

2. Tom Rouen and Jake Plummer

3. Bradley Roby and Howard Griffith

4. Ron Leary and Gary Zimmerman

5. Karl Mecklenburg and Lyle Alzado

6. Steve Watson and Owen Daniels

7. Bubby Brister and Jay Cutler

8. Ed McCaffrey and Eric Decker

9. Evan Mathis and Mark Schlereth

10. T.J. Ward and Steve Foley

11. Brian Griese and Brandon Stokley

12. Demaryius Thomas and Riley Odoms

13. Harald Hasselbach and Mitch Unrein

14. DeMarcus Ware and Domata Peko Sr.

15. Dwayne Carswell and Daniel Graham

16. Wes Welker and Anthony Miller

17. Rulon Jones and Brian Habib

18. Danny Trevathan and Glenn Cadrez

19. Will Parks and Tyrone Braxton

20. Aaron Brewer and Spencer Larsen

Quiz 21: Answers

1. Von Miller 2. Knowshon Moreno 3. Ryan Clady 4. Brown 5. Tuesday and Wednesday 6. Dennis Smith 7. DeMarcus Ware 8. Arizona 9. New England 10. Todd Sauerbrun 11. Ronnie Hillman 12. Rod Smith and Demaryius Thomas 13. Omaha 14. Steve Atwater, Shannon Sharpe and Demaryius Thomas 15. Emmanuel Sanders 16. Dallas 17. Owen Daniels 18. True 19. c) 77,160 20. c) Green Bay

Quiz 23: Pot Luck

1. Before being appointed head coach in Denver Vance Joseph had been the defensive coordinator at which team?

2. Von Miller wears the jersey number that he does in honor of which legendary pass rusher?

3. The last time the Broncos had two players gain over 100 rushing yards in the same game was in 2011. Who were the two players?

4. The Broncos have won more games in which month than any other?

5. Who are the two Broncos with over 250 combined rushing and receiving yards in a single game?

6. Since its inception in 1986, who is the only Denver safety to have been named AFC Defensive Player of the Month?

7. In 2018, the Broncos sent Aqib Talib to which team in exchange for a fifth-round draft pick?

8. True or false – the Broncos were the first team that started life in the AFL to record 400 franchise wins?

9. Of Denver backs with at least 100 rushing attempts, who has the best yards per carry average in a single season?

10. In the ten seasons between 2007 and 2016 the Broncos had just two backs who rushed for 1,000 yards in a season. Which two?

11. Which pair of receivers combined for a league-best 2,718 yards in 2013?

12. During the 1990s the Broncos had four running backs who rushed for 1,000 yards in a season. Name the quartet.

13. Who was the last tight end to lead the team in yards per catch average in a season (minimum 20 receptions)?

14. Which barefoot kicker led the Broncos in points scored for seven straight seasons between 1982 and 1988?

15. Which offensive lineman appeared in 166 consecutive games for the Broncos between 1981 and 1992?

16. Who holds the franchise record for the best gross punting average in a single season at 47.4 yards per punt?

17. Who are the three Denver quarterbacks to have thrown over 35 passes in a game in their rookie season?

18. Which two Super Bowl 50 starters for the Broncos have surnames that end in a vowel?

19. What type of grass is used for the field at Broncos Stadium at Mile High? a) Alabama Bluegrass b) Kentucky Bluegrass c) Louisiana Bluegrass

20. Who is the only Denver wide receiver to have been named AFC Offensive Player of the Month? a) Vance Johnson b) Ed McCaffrey c) Rod Smith

Quiz 22: Answers

1. #24 2. #16 3. #29 4. #65 5. #77 6. #81 7. #6 8. #87 9. #69 10. #43 11. #14 12. #88 13. #96 14. #94 15. #89 16. #83 17. #75 18. #59 19. #34 20. #46

Quiz 24: Anagrams

Re-arrange the letters to make the name of a current or former Broncos players or coach.

1. I Grub Kayak

2. Seek Acumen

3. Imparts Data

4. Rockier Elbows

5. Arched Bubbly

6. Mercenary Foe

7. Radiant Waters

8. Read Seven

9. Scorned Jan

10. Folder Week

11. Shy Arena

12. Orderly Baby

13. Folly Tilted

14. Dish Radar Angry

15. Man Has Hankie

16. Now Onshore Monk

17. Lead Slip Whip

18. No Skim Jackal

19. Global Street

20. Ran Buns Command

Quiz 23: Answers

1. Miami 2. Derrick Thomas 3. Willis McGahee and Tim Tebow 4. October 5. Mike Anderson and Clinton Portis 6. Dennis Smith 7. L.A. Rams 8. False (they were the second) 9. Clinton Portis 10. Willis McGahee and Knowshon Moreno 11. Demaryius Thomas and Eric Decker 12. Bobby Humphrey, Gaston Green, Terrell Davis and Olandis Gary 13. Tony Scheffler 14. Rich Karlis 15. Ken Lanier 16. Britton Colquitt 17. John Elway, Tim Tebow and Paxton Lynch 18. Derek Wolfe and DeMarcus Ware 19. Kentucky Bluegrass 20. c) Rod Smith

Quiz 25: Pot Luck

1. Who was the last safety selected by the Broncos in the first round of the NFL Draft?

2. Bill Kollar is the coach of which position group?

3. True or false – the Broncos won every opening game of the season between 2012 and 2018?

4. The 'Good Guy' award given annually to a Denver player and decided by the local media is named after which former Bronco?

5. Who are the two Denver cornerbacks to have the won the AFC Defensive Play of the Month Award?

6. Who was the last Bronco to record over 200 tackles in a single season?

7. Who holds the record for the most interception return touchdowns in franchise history?

8. Before Phillip Lindsay who was the last Bronco to wear the number 30 jersey?

9. True or false – Chris Harris Jr's middle name is Columbus?

10. Which defensive back returned two interceptions for touchdowns during the 2016 season?

11. Prior to the start of the 2018 season, who was the last Bronco to score double-digit touchdowns in a single season?

12. What number jersey is worn by wide receiver Courtland Sutton?

13. True or false – Gary Kubiak was the first player in NFL history to win the Super Bowl with the same team both as a player and a head coach?

14. Does Von Miller wear glasses or contact lenses during games?

15. Who started at left tackle in all 19 games during the 2015 World Championship season?

16. Which kicker received AFC Special Teams Player of the Month honors in both 2009 and 2011?

17. Sturdy run stuffer Domata Peko spent the first 11 years of his NFL career with which team?

18. Which safety picked off a Tom Brady pass in the 2015 AFC Championship game?

19. By what name was running back Carlton Gilchrist better known? a) Candy b) Chip c) Cookie

20. How many regular season-starts did John Elway make for the Broncos? a) 211 b) 221 c) 231

Quiz 24: Answers

1. Gary Kubiak 2. Case Keenum 3. Matt Paradis 4. Brock Osweiler 5. Bradley Chubb 6. Royce Freeman 7. Darian Stewart 8. Dan Reeves 9. C.J. Anderson 10. Derek Wolfe 11. Shane Ray 12. Bradley Roby 13. Floyd Little 14. Randy Gradishar 15. Mike Shanahan 16. Knowshon Moreno 17. Wade Phillips 18. Malik Jackson 19. Garett Bolles 20. Brandon McManus

Made in the USA
Coppell, TX
18 June 2020